Mabel Loomis Todd, Emily Dickinson

Poems

Third Series

Mabel Loomis Todd, Emily Dickinson

Poems
Third Series

ISBN/EAN: 9783744713993

Printed in Europe, USA, Canada, Australia, Japan

Cover: Foto ©Thomas Meinert / pixelio.de

More available books at **www.hansebooks.com**

POEMS

BY

EMILY DICKINSON

THIRD SERIES

POEMS

BY

EMILY DICKINSON

Edited by

MABEL LOOMIS TODD

THIRD SERIES

BOSTON
ROBERTS BROTHERS
1896

Copyright, 1896,
By Roberts Brothers.

SECOND EDITION.

University Press:
John Wilson and Son, Cambridge, U. S. A.

IT 's all I have to bring to-day,
  This, and my heart beside,
This, and my heart, and all the fields,
  And all the meadows wide.
Be sure you count, should I forget, —
  Some one the sum could tell, —
This, and my heart, and all the bees
  Which in the clover dwell.

PREFACE.

THE intellectual activity of Emily Dickinson was so great that a large and characteristic choice is still possible among her literary material, and this third volume of her verses is put forth in response to the repeated wish of the admirers of her peculiar genius.

Much of Emily Dickinson's prose was rhythmic, — even rhymed, though frequently not set apart in lines. Also many verses, written as such, were sent to friends in letters; these were published in 1894, in the volumes of her *Letters*. It has not been necessary, however, to include them in this Series, and all have been omitted, except three or four exceptionally strong ones, as "A Book," and "With Flowers."

There is internal evidence that many of the poems were simply spontaneous flashes of insight, apparently unrelated to outward circumstance. Others, however, had an obvious personal origin; for example, the verses "I had a Guinea golden," which seem to have been sent to some friend travelling in Europe, as a dainty reminder of letter-writing delinquencies. The surroundings in which any of Emily Dickinson's verses are known to have been written usually serve to explain them clearly; but in general the present volume is full of thoughts needing no interpretation to those who apprehend this scintillating spirit.

M. L. T.

AMHERST, *October*, 1896.

CONTENTS.

Prelude v
Preface vii

BOOK I.—LIFE.

		Page
I.	Real Riches	13
II.	Superiority to Fate	14
III.	Hope	15
IV.	Forbidden Fruit (1)	16
V.	Forbidden Fruit (2)	17
VI.	A Word	18
VII.	"To venerate the simple days" . . .	19
VIII.	Life's Trades	20
IX.	"Drowning is not so pitiful"	21
X.	"How still the bells in steeples stand"	22
XI.	"If the foolish call them 'flowers'"	23
XII.	A Syllable	25

CONTENTS.

		PAGE
XIII.	Parting	26
XIV.	Aspiration	27
XV.	The Inevitable	28
XVI.	A Book	29
XVII.	"Who has not found the heaven below"	30
XVIII.	A Portrait	31
XIX.	I had a Guinea Golden	32
XX.	Saturday Afternoon	34
XXI.	"Few get enough, — enough is one"	35
XXII.	"Upon the gallows hung a wretch"	36
XXIII.	The Lost Thought	37
XXIV.	Reticence	38
XXV.	With Flowers	39
XXVI.	"The farthest thunder that I heard"	40
XXVII.	"On the bleakness of my lot"	41
XXVIII.	Contrast	42
XXIX.	Friends	43
XXX.	Fire	44
XXXI.	A Man	45
XXXII.	Ventures	46
XXXIII.	Griefs	47
XXXIV.	"I have a king who does not speak"	49

CONTENTS.

		PAGE
XXXV.	Disenchantment	50
XXXVI.	Lost Faith	51
XXXVII.	Lost Joy	52
XXXVIII.	"I worked for chaff, and earning wheat"	53
XXXIX.	"Life, and Death, and Giants"	54
XL.	Alpine Glow	55
XLI.	Remembrance	56
XLII.	"To hang our head ostensibly"	57
XLIII.	The Brain	58
XLIV.	"The bone that has no marrow"	59
XLV.	The Past	60
XLVI.	"To help our bleaker parts"	61
XLVII.	"What soft, cherubic creatures"	62
XLVIII.	Desire	63
XLIX.	Philosophy	64
L.	Power	65
LI.	"A modest lot, a fame *petite*"	66
LII.	"Is bliss, then, such abyss"	67
LIII.	Experience	68
LIV.	Thanksgiving Day	69
LV.	Childish Griefs	70

CONTENTS.

BOOK II. — LOVE.

		PAGE
I.	Consecration	73
II.	Love's Humility	74
III.	Love	75
IV.	Satisfied	76
V.	With a Flower	78
VI.	Song	79
VII.	Loyalty	80
VIII.	"To lose thee, sweeter than to gain"	81
IX.	"Poor little heart!"	82
X.	Forgotten	83
XI.	"I've got an arrow here"	85
XII.	The Master	86
XIII.	"Heart, we will forget him!"	87
XIV.	"Father, I bring thee not myself"	88
XV.	"We outgrow love, like other things"	89
XVI.	"Not with a club the heart is broken"	90
XVII.	Who?	91
XVIII.	"He touched me, so I live to know"	92
XIX.	Dreams	93
XX.	Numen Lumen	94

CONTENTS.

		PAGE
XXI.	Longing	95
XXII.	Wedded	97

BOOK III.—NATURE.

I.	Nature's Changes	101
II.	The Tulip	102
III.	"A light exists in spring"	103
IV.	The Waking Year	105
V.	To March	106
VI.	March	108
VII.	Dawn	109
VIII.	"A murmur in the trees to note"	110
IX.	"Morning is the place for dew"	112
X.	"To my quick ears the leaves conferred"	113
XI.	A Rose	114
XII.	"High from the earth I heard a bird"	115
XIII.	Cobwebs	116
XIV.	A Well	117
XV.	"To make a prairie it takes a clover"	119
XVI.	The Wind	120
XVII.	"A dew sufficed itself"	121

		PAGE
XVIII.	The Woodpecker	122
XIX.	A Snake	123
XX.	"Could I but ride indefinite"	124
XXI.	The Moon	125
XXII.	The Bat	127
XXIII.	The Balloon	128
XXIV.	Evening	130
XXV.	Cocoon	131
XXVI.	Sunset	132
XXVII.	Aurora	133
XXVIII.	The Coming of Night	134
XXIX.	Aftermath	136

BOOK IV.—TIME AND ETERNITY.

I.	"This world is not conclusion"	139
II.	"We learn in the retreating"	140
III.	"They say that 'time assuages'"	141
IV.	"We cover thee, sweet face"	142
V.	Ending	143
VI.	"The stimulus, beyond the grave"	144
VII.	"Given in marriage unto thee"	145

CONTENTS.

		PAGE
VIII.	"That such have died enables us"	146
IX.	"They won't frown always, — some sweet day"	147
X.	Immortality	148
XI.	"The distance that the dead have gone"	149
XII.	"How dare the robins sing"	150
XIII.	Death	151
XIV.	Unwarned	152
XV.	"Each that we lose takes part of us"	153
XVI.	"Not any higher stands the grave"	154
XVII.	Asleep	155
XVIII.	The Spirit	156
XIX.	The Monument	157
XX.	"Bless God, he went as soldiers"	158
XXI.	"Immortal is an ample word"	159
XXII.	"Where every bird is bold to go"	160
XXIII.	"The grave my little cottage is"	161
XXIV.	"This was in the white of the year"	162
XXV.	"Sweet hours have perished here"	163
XXVI.	"Me! Come! My dazzled face"	164
XXVII.	Invisible	165
XXVIII.	"I wish I knew that woman's name"	166

CONTENTS.

		PAGE
XXIX.	Trying to Forget	167
XXX.	"I felt a funeral in my brain"	168
XXXI.	"I meant to find her when I came"	169
XXXII.	Waiting	170
XXXIII.	"A sickness of this world it most occasions"	171
XXXIV.	"Superfluous were the sun"	172
XXXV.	"So proud she was to die"	173
XXXVI.	Farewell	174
XXXVII.	"The dying need but little, dear"	175
XXXVIII.	Dead	176
XXXIX.	"The soul should always stand ajar"	177
XL.	"Three weeks passed since I had seen her"	178
XLI.	"I breathed enough to learn the trick"	179
XLII.	"I wonder if the sepulchre"	180
XLIII.	Joy in Death	181
XLIV.	"If I may have it when it's dead"	182
XLV.	"Before the ice is in the pools"	183
XLVI.	Dying	184
XLVII.	"Adrift! A little boat adrift!"	185
XLVIII.	"There's been a death in the opposite house"	186
XLIX.	"We never know we go, — when we are going"	188

CONTENTS.

		PAGE
L.	The Soul's Storm	189
LI.	"Water is taught by thirst"	190
LII.	Thirst	191
LIII.	"A clock stopped — not the mantel's"	192
LIV.	Charlotte Brontë's Grave	193
LV.	"A toad can die of light!"	195
LVI.	"Far from love the Heavenly Father"	196
LVII.	Sleeping	197
LVIII.	Retrospect	198
LIX.	Eternity	200

# I.

LIFE.

POEMS.

I.

REAL RICHES.

'TIS little I could care for pearls
　　Who own the ample sea;
Or brooches, when the Emperor
　　With rubies pelteth me;

Or gold, who am the Prince of Mines;
　　Or diamonds, when I see
A diadem to fit a dome
　　Continual crowning me.

II.

SUPERIORITY TO FATE.

SUPERIORITY to fate
   Is difficult to learn.
'T is not conferred by any,
   But possible to earn

A pittance at a time,
   Until, to her surprise,
The soul with strict economy
   Subsists till Paradise.

III.

HOPE.

HOPE is a subtle glutton;
    He feeds upon the fair;
And yet, inspected closely,
    What abstinence is there!

His is the halcyon table
    That never seats but one,
And whatsoever is consumed
    The same amounts remain.

IV.

FORBIDDEN FRUIT.

I.

FORBIDDEN fruit a flavor has
    That lawful orchards mocks;
How luscious lies the pea within
The pod that Duty locks!

V.

FORBIDDEN FRUIT.

II.

HEAVEN is what I cannot reach!
   The apple on the tree,
Provided it do hopeless hang,
   That 'heaven' is, to me.

The color on the cruising cloud,
   The interdicted ground
Behind the hill, the house behind, —
   There Paradise is found!

VI.

A WORD.

A WORD is dead
   When it is said,
  Some say.
I say it just
Begins to live
  That day.

VII.

To venerate the simple days
  Which lead the seasons by,
Needs but to remember
  That from you or me
They may take the trifle
  Termed mortality!

To invest existence with a stately air,
Needs but to remember
  That the acorn there
Is the egg of forests
  For the upper air!

VIII.

LIFE'S TRADES.

I T 's such a little thing to weep,
    So short a thing to sigh ;
And yet by trades the size of these
We men and women die !

IX.

DROWNING is not so pitiful
   As the attempt to rise.
Three times, 't is said, a sinking man
   Comes up to face the skies,
And then declines forever
   To that abhorred abode
Where hope and he part company, —
   For he is grasped of God.
The Maker's cordial visage,
   However good to see,
Is shunned, we must admit it,
   Like an adversity.

X.

How still the bells in steeples stand,
    Till, swollen with the sky,
They leap upon their silver feet
    In frantic melody!

XI.

IF the foolish call them 'flowers,'
    Need the wiser tell?
If the savans 'classify' them,
    It is just as well!

Those who read the *Revelations*
    Must not criticise
Those who read the same edition
    With beclouded eyes!

Could we stand with that old Moses
    Canaan denied, —
Scan, like him, the stately landscape
    On the other side, —

Doubtless we should deem superfluous
    Many sciences
Not pursued by learnèd angels
    In scholastic skies!

Low amid that glad *Belles lettres*
    Grant that we may stand,
Stars, amid profound Galaxies,
    At that grand 'Right hand'!

XII.

A SYLLABLE.

COULD mortal lip divine
   The undeveloped freight
Of a delivered syllable,
   'T would crumble with the weight.

XIII.

PARTING.

My life closed twice before its close;
    It yet remains to see
If Immortality unveil
    A third event to me,

So huge, so hopeless to conceive,
    As these that twice befell.
Parting is all we know of heaven,
    And all we need of hell.

XIV.

ASPIRATION.

WE never know how high we are
    Till we are called to rise;
And then, if we are true to plan,
    Our statures touch the skies.

The heroism we recite
    Would be a daily thing,
Did not ourselves the cubits warp
    For fear to be a king.

XV.

THE INEVITABLE.

While I was fearing it, it came,
    But came with less of fear,
Because that fearing it so long
    Had almost made it dear.
There is a fitting a dismay,
    A fitting a despair.
'Tis harder knowing it is due,
    Than knowing it is here.
The trying on the utmost,
    The morning it is new,
Is terribler than wearing it
    A whole existence through.

XVI.

A BOOK.

THERE is no frigate like a book
    To take us lands away,
Nor any coursers like a page
    Of prancing poetry.
This traverse may the poorest take
    Without oppress of toll;
How frugal is the chariot
    That bears a human soul!

XVII.

WHO has not found the heaven below
    Will fail of it above.
God's residence is next to mine,
    His furniture is love.

XVIII.

A PORTRAIT.

A FACE devoid of love or grace,
   A hateful, hard, successful face,
A face with which a stone
Would feel as thoroughly at ease
As were they old acquaintances, —
   First time together thrown.

XIX.

I HAD A GUINEA GOLDEN.

I HAD a guinea golden;
　　I lost it in the sand,
And though the sum was simple,
　　And pounds were in the land,
Still had it such a value
　　Unto my frugal eye,
That when I could not find it
　　I sat me down to sigh.

I had a crimson robin
　　Who sang full many a day,
But when the woods were painted
　　He, too, did fly away.
Time brought me other robins, —
　　Their ballads were the same, —
Still for my missing troubadour
　　I kept the 'house at hame.'

I had a star in heaven ;
  One Pleiad was its name,
And when I was not heeding
  It wandered from the same.
And though the skies are crowded,
  And all the night ashine,
I do not care about it,
  Since none of them are mine.

My story has a moral :
  I have a missing friend, —
Pleiad its name, and robin,
  And guinea in the sand, —
And when this mournful ditty,
  Accompanied with tear,
Shall meet the eye of traitor
  In country far from here,
Grant that repentance solemn
  May seize upon his mind,
And he no consolation
  Beneath the sun may find.

NOTE. — This poem may have had, like many others, a personal origin. It is more than probable that it was sent to some friend travelling in Europe, a dainty reminder of letter-writing delinquencies.

XX.

SATURDAY AFTERNOON.

FROM all the jails the boys and girls
    Ecstatically leap, —
Beloved, only afternoon
    That prison does n't keep.

They storm the earth and stun the air,
    A mob of solid bliss.
Alas! that frowns could lie in wait
    For such a foe as this!

XXI.

FEW get enough, — enough is one;
  To that ethereal throng
Have not each one of us the right
  To stealthily belong?

XXII.

UPON the gallows hung a wretch,
    Too sullied for the hell
To which the law entitled him.
    As nature's curtain fell
The one who bore him tottered in,
    For this was woman's son.
' 'T was all I had,' she stricken gasped;
    Oh, what a livid boon!

XXIII.

THE LOST THOUGHT.

I FELT a clearing in my mind
   As if my brain had split;
I tried to match it, seam by seam,
   But could not make them fit.

The thought behind I strove to join
   Unto the thought before,
But sequence ravelled out of reach
   Like balls upon a floor.

XXIV.

RETICENCE.

THE reticent volcano keeps
    His never slumbering plan;
Confided are his projects pink
    To no precarious man.

If nature will not tell the tale
    Jehovah told to her,
Can human nature not survive
    Without a listener?

Admonished by her buckled lips
    Let every babbler be.
The only secret people keep
    Is Immortality.

XXV.

WITH FLOWERS.

IF recollecting were forgetting,
   Then I remember not;
And if forgetting, recollecting,
   How near I had forgot!
And if to miss were merry,
   And if to mourn were gay,
How very blithe the fingers
   That gathered these to-day!

XXVI.

THE farthest thunder that I heard
    Was nearer than the sky,
And rumbles still, though torrid noons
    Have lain their missiles by.
The lightning that preceded it
    Struck no one but myself,
But I would not exchange the bolt
    For all the rest of life.
Indebtedness to oxygen
    The chemist may repay,
But not the obligation
    To electricity.
It founds the homes and decks the days,
    And every clamor bright
Is but the gleam concomitant
    Of that waylaying light.
The thought is quiet as a flake, —
    A crash without a sound;
How life's reverberation
    Its explanation found!

XXVII.

ON the bleakness of my lot
    Bloom I strove to raise.
Late, my acre of a rock
    Yielded grape and maize.

Soil of flint if steadfast tilled
    Will reward the hand;
Seed of palm by Lybian sun
    Fructified in sand.

XXVIII.

CONTRAST.

A DOOR just opened on a street —
    I, lost, was passing by —
An instant's width of warmth disclosed,
    And wealth, and company.

The door as sudden shut, and I,
    I, lost, was passing by, —
Lost doubly, but by contrast most,
    Enlightening misery.

XXIX.

FRIENDS.

ARE friends delight or pain?
 Could bounty but remain
Riches were good.

But if they only stay
Bolder to fly away,
 Riches are sad.

XXX.

FIRE.

Ashes denote that fire was;
    Respect the grayest pile
For the departed creature's sake
    That hovered there awhile.

Fire exists the first in light,
    And then consolidates, —
Only the chemist can disclose
    Into what carbonates.

XXXI.

A MAN.

FATE slew him, but he did not drop;
   She felled — he did not fall —
Impaled him on her fiercest stakes —
   He neutralized them all.

She stung him, sapped his firm advance,
   But, when her worst was done,
And he, unmoved, regarded her,
   Acknowledged him a man.

XXXII.

VENTURES.

FINITE to fail, but infinite to venture.
   For the one ship that struts the shore
Many 's the gallant, overwhelmed creature
Nodding in navies nevermore.

XXXIII.

GRIEFS.

I MEASURE every grief I meet
  With analytic eyes;
I wonder if it weighs like mine,
  Or has an easier size.

I wonder if they bore it long,
  Or did it jùst begin?
I could not tell the date of mine,
  It feels so old a pain.

I wonder if it hurts to live,
  And if they have to try,
And whether, could they choose between,
  They would not rather die.

I wonder if when years have piled —
  Some thousands — on the cause
Of early hurt, if such a lapse
  Could give them any pause;

Or would they go on aching still
    Through centuries above,
Enlightened to a larger pain
    By contrast with the love.

The grieved are many, I am told;
    The reason deeper lies, —
Death is but one and comes but once,
    And only nails the eyes.

There 's grief of want, and grief of cold, —
    A sort they call 'despair;'
There 's banishment from native eyes,
    In sight of native air.

And though I may not guess the kind
    Correctly, yet to me
A piercing comfort it affords
    In passing Calvary,

To note the fashions of the cross,
    Of those that stand alone,
Still fascinated to presume
    That some are like my own.

XXXIV.

I HAVE a king who does not speak;
　So, wondering, thro' the hours meek
I trudge the day away, —
Half glad when it is night and sleep,
If, haply, thro' a dream to peep
　In parlors shut by day.

And if I do, when morning comes,
It is as if a hundred drums
　Did round my pillow roll,
And shouts fill all my childish sky,
And bells keep saying 'victory'
　From steeples in my soul!

And if I don't, the little Bird
Within the Orchard is not heard,
　And I omit to pray,
'Father, thy will be done' to-day,
For my will goes the other way,
　And it were perjury!

XXXV.

DISENCHANTMENT.

IT dropped so low in my regard
    I heard it hit the ground,
And go to pieces on the stones
    At bottom of my mind;

Yet blamed the fate that fractured, less
    Than I reviled myself
For entertaining plated wares
    Upon my silver shelf.

XXXVI.

LOST FAITH.

TO lose one's faith surpasses
  The loss of an estate,
Because estates can be
  Replenished, — faith cannot.

Inherited with life,
  Belief but once can be;
Annihilate a single clause,
  And Being's beggary.

XXXVII.

LOST JOY.

I HAD a daily bliss
    I half indifferent viewed,
Till sudden I perceived it stir, —
    It grew as I pursued,

Till when, around a crag,
    It wasted from my sight,
Enlarged beyond my utmost scope,
    I learned its sweetness right.

XXXVIII.

I WORKED for chaff, and earning wheat
  Was haughty and betrayed.
What right had fields to arbitrate
  In matters ratified?

I tasted wheat, — and hated chaff,
  And thanked the ample friend;
Wisdom is more becoming viewed
  At distance than at hand.

XXXIX.

LIFE, and Death, and Giants
    Such as these, are still.
Minor apparatus, hopper of the mill,
Beetle at the candle,
    Or a fife's small fame,
Maintain by accident
    That they proclaim.

XL.

ALPINE GLOW.

OUR lives are Swiss, —
   So still, so cool,
Till, some odd afternoon,
The Alps neglect their curtains,
   And we look farther on.

Italy stands the other side,
   While, like a guard between,
The solemn Alps,
The siren Alps,
   Forever intervene !

XLI.

REMEMBRANCE.

REMEMBRANCE has a rear and front, —
  'T is something like a house;
It has a garret also
  For refuse and the mouse,

Besides, the deepest cellar
  That ever mason hewed;
Look to it, by its fathoms
  Ourselves be not pursued.

XLII.

To hang our head ostensibly,
    And subsequent to find
That such was not the posture
    Of our immortal mind,

Affords the sly presumption
    That, in so dense a fuzz,
You, too, take cobweb attitudes
    Upon a plane of gauze !

XLIII.

THE BRAIN.

THE brain is wider than the sky,
    For, put them side by side,
The one the other will include
    With ease, and you beside.

The brain is deeper than the sea,
    For, hold them, blue to blue,
The one the other will absorb,
    As sponges, buckets do.

The brain is just the weight of God,
    For, lift them, pound for pound,
And they will differ, if they do,
    As syllable from sound.

XLIV.

THE bone that has no marrow;
    What ultimate for that?
It is not fit for table,
    For beggar, or for cat.

A bone has obligations,
    A being has the same;
A marrowless assembly
    Is culpabler than shame.

But how shall finished creatures
    A function fresh obtain? —
Old Nicodemus' phantom
    Confronting us again!

XLV.

THE PAST.

The past is such a curious creature,
    To look her in the face
A transport may reward us,
    Or a disgrace.

Unarmed if any meet her,
    I charge him, fly!
Her rusty ammunition
    Might yet reply!

XLVI.

To help our bleaker parts
  Salubrious hours are given,
Which if they do not fit for earth
  Drill silently for heaven.

XLVII.

WHAT soft, cherubic creatures
    These gentlewomen are!
One would as soon assault a plush
    Or violate a star.

Such dimity convictions,
    A horror so refined
Of freckled human nature,
    Of Deity ashamed, —

It's such a common glory,
    A fisherman's degree!
Redemption, brittle lady,
    Be so, ashamed of thee.

XLVIII.

DESIRE.

WHO never wanted,— maddest joy
   Remains to him unknown;
The banquet of abstemiousness
   Surpasses that of wine.

Within its hope, though yet ungrasped
   Desire's perfect goal,
No nearer, lest reality
   Should disenthrall thy soul.

XLIX.

PHILOSOPHY.

IT might be easier
    To fail with land in sight,
Than gain my blue peninsula
To perish of delight.

L.

POWER.

YOU cannot put a fire out;
   A thing that can ignite
Can go, itself, without a fan
   Upon the slowest night.

You cannot fold a flood
   And put it in a drawer, —
Because the winds would find it out,
   And tell your cedar floor.

LI.

A MODEST lot, a fame *petite*,
    A brief campaign of sting and sweet
Is plenty ! Is enough !
A sailor's business is the shore,
    A soldier's — balls. Who asketh more
Must seek the neighboring life !

LII.

IS bliss, then, such abyss
    I must not put my foot amiss
For fear I spoil my shoe?

I 'd rather suit my foot
Than save my boot,
For yet to buy another pair
Is possible
At any fair.

But bliss is sold just once;
The patent lost
None buy it any more.

LIII.

EXPERIENCE.

I STEPPED from plank to plank
    So slow and cautiously;
The stars about my head I felt,
    About my feet the sea.

I knew not but the next
    Would be my final inch, —
This gave me that precarious gait
    Some call experience.

LIV.

THANKSGIVING DAY.

ONE day is there of the series
    Termed Thanksgiving day,
Celebrated part at table,
    Part in memory.

Neither patriarch nor pussy,
    I dissect the play;
Seems it, to my hooded thinking,
    Reflex holiday.

Had there been no sharp subtraction
    From the early sum,
Not an acre or a caption
    Where was once a room,

Not a mention, whose small pebble
    Wrinkled any bay, —
Unto such, were such assembly,
    'T were Thanksgiving day.

LV.

CHILDISH GRIEFS.

SOFTENED by Time's consummate plush,
    How sleek the woe appears
That threatened childhood's citadel
    And undermined the years!

Bisected now by bleaker griefs,
    We envy the despair
That devastated childhood's realm,
    So easy to repair.

II.

LOVE.

I.

CONSECRATION.

Proud of my broken heart since thou didst break it,
  Proud of the pain I did not feel till thee,
Proud of my night since thou with moons dost slake it,
  Not to partake thy passion, my humility.

II.

LOVE'S HUMILITY.

MY worthiness is all my doubt,
   His merit all my fear,
Contrasting which, my qualities
   Do lowlier appear;

Lest I should insufficient prove
   For his beloved need,
The chiefest apprehension
   Within my loving creed.

So I, the undivine abode
   Of his elect content,
Conform my soul as 't were a church
   Unto her sacrament.

III.

LOVE.

LOVE is anterior to life,
  Posterior to death,
Initial of creation, and
  The exponent of breath.

IV.

SATISFIED.

ONE blessing had I, than the rest
    So larger to my eyes
That I stopped gauging, satisfied,
    For this enchanted size.

It was the limit of my dream,
    The focus of my prayer, —
A perfect, paralyzing bliss
    Contented as despair.

I knew no more of want or cold,
    Phantasms both become,
For this new value in the soul,
    Supremest earthly sum.

The heaven below the heaven above
    Obscured with ruddier hue.
Life's latitude leant over-full;
    The judgment perished, too.

Why joys so scantily disburse,
   Why Paradise defer,
Why floods are served to us in bowls, —
   I speculate no more.

V.

WITH A FLOWER.

WHEN roses cease to bloom, dear,
    And violets are done,
When bumble-bees in solemn flight
    Have passed beyond the sun,

The hand that paused to gather
    Upon this summer's day
Will idle lie, in Auburn, —
    Then take my flower, pray!

VI.

SONG.

SUMMER for thee grant I may be
   When summer days are flown!
Thy music still when whippoorwill
   And oriole are done!

For thee to bloom, I'll skip the tomb
   And sow my blossoms o'er!
Pray gather me, Anemone,
   Thy flower forevermore!

VII.

LOYALTY.

SPLIT the lark and you 'll find the music,
   Bulb after bulb, in silver rolled,
Scantily dealt to the summer morning,
   Saved for your ear when lutes be old.

Loose the flood, you shall find it patent,
   Gush after gush, reserved for you;
Scarlet experiment! sceptic Thomas,
   Now, do you doubt that your bird was true?

VIII.

TO lose thee, sweeter than to gain
    All other hearts I knew.
'T is true the drought is destitute,
    But then I had the dew!

The Caspian has its realms of sand,
    Its other realm of sea;
Without the sterile perquisite
    No Caspian could be.

IX.

Poor little heart!
    Did they forget thee?
Then dinna care! Then dinna care!

Proud little heart!
Did they forsake thee?
Be debonair! Be debonair!

Frail little heart!
I would not break thee:
Could'st credit me? Could'st credit me?

Gay little heart!
Like morning glory
Thou'll wilted be; thou'll wilted be!

X.

FORGOTTEN.

THERE is a word
   Which bears a sword
  Can pierce an armed man.
It hurls its barbed syllables, —
  At once is mute again.
But where it fell
The saved will tell
  On patriotic day,
Some epauletted brother
  Gave his breath away.

Wherever runs the breathless sun,
  Wherever roams the day,
There is its noiseless onset,
  There is its victory!

Behold the keenest marksman!
　The most accomplished shot!
Time's sublimest target
　Is a soul 'forgot'!

XI.

I 'VE got an arrow here;
   Loving the hand that sent it,
I the dart revere.

Fell, they will say, in 'skirmish'!
   Vanquished, my soul will know,
By but a simple arrow
   Sped by an archer's bow.

XII.

THE MASTER.

He fumbles at your spirit
    As players at the keys
Before they drop full music on;
    He stuns you by degrees,

Prepares your brittle substance
    For the ethereal blow,
By fainter hammers, further heard,
    Then nearer, then so slow

Your breath has time to straighten,
    Your brain to bubble cool, —
Deals one imperial thunderbolt
    That scalps your naked soul.

XIII.

HEART, we will forget him!
   You and I, to-night!
You may forget the warmth he gave,
   I will forget the light.

When you have done, pray tell me,
   That I my thoughts may dim;
Haste! lest while you 're lagging,
   I may remember him!

XIV.

FATHER, I bring thee not myself, —
  That were the little load;
I bring thee the imperial heart
  I had not strength to hold.

The heart I cherished in my own
  Till mine too heavy grew,
Yet strangest, heavier since it went,
  Is it too large for you?

XV.

WE outgrow love like other things
 And put it in the drawer,
Till it an antique fashion shows
 Like costumes grandsires wore.

XVI.

NOT with a club the heart is broken,
    Nor with a stone;
A whip, so small you could not see it,
    I 've known

To lash the magic creature
    Till it fell,
Yet that whip's name too noble
    Then to tell.

Magnanimous of bird
    By boy descried,
To sing unto the stone
    Of which it died.

XVII.

WHO?

MY friend must be a bird,
    Because it flies!
Mortal my friend must be,
    Because it dies!
Barbs has it, like a bee.
Ah, curious friend,
    Thou puzzlest me!

XVIII.

He touched me, so I live to know
    That such a day, permitted so,
  I groped upon his breast.
It was a boundless place to me,
And silenced, as the awful sea
  Puts minor streams to rest.

And now, I'm different from before,
As if I breathed superior air,
  Or brushed a royal gown;
My feet, too, that had wandered so,
My gypsy face transfigured now
  To tenderer renown.

XIX.

DREAMS.

Let me not mar that perfect dream
　　By an auroral stain,
But so adjust my daily night
　　That it will come again.

XX.

NUMEN LUMEN.

I LIVE with him, I see his face;
   I go no more away
For visitor, or sundown;
   Death's single privacy,

The only one forestalling mine,
   And that by right that he
Presents a claim invisible,
   No wedlock granted me.

I live with him, I hear his voice,
   I stand alive to-day
To witness to the certainty
   Of immortality

Taught me by Time, — the lower way,
   Conviction every day, —
That life like this is endless,
   Be judgment what it may.

XXI.

LONGING.

I ENVY seas whereon he rides,
   I envy spokes of wheels
Of chariots that him convey,
   I envy speechless hills

That gaze upon his journey;
   How easy all can see
What is forbidden utterly
   As heaven, unto me!

I envy nests of sparrows
   That dot his distant eaves,
The wealthy fly upon his pane,
   The happy, happy leaves

That just abroad his window
   Have summer's leave to be,
The earrings of Pizarro
   Could not obtain for me.

I envy light that wakes him,
   And bells that boldly ring
To tell him it is noon abroad, —
   Myself his noon could bring,

Yet interdict my blossom
   And abrogate my bee,
Lest noon in everlasting night
   Drop Gabriel and me.

XXII.

WEDDED.

A SOLEMN thing it was, I said,
   A woman white to be,
And wear, if God should count me fit,
   Her hallowed mystery.

A timid thing to drop a life
   Into the purple well,
Too plummetless that it come back
   Eternity until.

III.

NATURE.

I.

NATURE'S CHANGES.

THE springtime's pallid landscape
  Will glow like bright bouquet,
Though drifted deep in parian
  The village lies to-day.

The lilacs, bending many a year,
  With purple load will hang;
The bees will not forget the tune
  Their old forefathers sang.

The rose will redden in the bog,
  The aster on the hill
Her everlasting fashion set,
  And covenant gentians frill,

Till summer folds her miracle
  As women do their gown,
Or priests adjust the symbols
  When sacrament is done.

II.

THE TULIP.

SHE slept beneath a tree
    Remembered but by me.
I touched her cradle mute ;
She recognized the foot,
Put on her carmine suit, —
    And see !

III.

A LIGHT exists in spring
   Not present on the year
At any other period.
   When March is scarcely here

A color stands abroad
   On solitary hills
That science cannot overtake,
   But human nature *feels*.

It waits upon the lawn;
   It shows the furthest tree
Upon the furthest slope we know;
   It almost speaks to me.

Then, as horizons step,
   Or noons report away,
Without the formula of sound,
   It passes, and we stay:

A quality of loss
  Affecting our content,
As trade had suddenly encroached
  Upon a sacrament.

IV.

THE WAKING YEAR.

A LADY red upon the hill
    Her annual secret keeps;
A lady white within the field
    In placid lily sleeps!

The tidy breezes with their brooms
    Sweep vale, and hill, and tree!
Prithee, my pretty housewives!
    Who may expected be?

The neighbors do not yet suspect!
    The woods exchange a smile —
Orchard, and buttercup, and bird —
    In such a little while!

And yet how still the landscape stands,
    How nonchalant the wood,
As if the resurrection
    Were nothing very odd!

V.

TO MARCH.

DEAR March, come in!
    How glad I am!
I looked for you before.
Put down your hat —
You must have walked —
How out of breath you are!
Dear March, how are you?
And the rest?
Did you leave Nature well?
Oh, March, come right upstairs with me,
I have so much to tell!

I got your letter, and the birds';
The maples never knew
That you were coming, — I declare,
How red their faces grew!
But, March, forgive me —
And all those hills

You left for me to hue;
There was no purple suitable,
You took it all with you.

Who knocks? That April!
Lock the door!
I will not be pursued!
He stayed away a year, to call
When I am occupied.
But trifles look so trivial
As soon as you have come,
That blame is just as dear as praise
And praise as mere as blame.

VI.

MARCH.

WE like March, his shoes are purple,
    He is new and high;
Makes he mud for dog and peddler,
    Makes he forest dry;
Knows the adder's tongue his coming,
    And begets her spot.
Stands the sun so close and mighty
    That our minds are hot.
News is he of all the others;
    Bold it were to die
With the blue-birds buccaneering
    On his British sky.

VII.

DAWN.

Not knowing when the dawn will come
  I open every door;
Or has it feathers like a bird,
  Or billows like a shore?

VIII.

A MURMUR in the trees to note,
    Not loud enough for wind;
A star not far enough to seek,
    Nor near enough to find;

A long, long yellow on the lawn,
    A hubbub as of feet;
Not audible, as ours to us,
    But dapperer, more sweet;

A hurrying home of little men
    To houses unperceived, —
All this, and more, if I should tell,
    Would never be believed.

Of robins in the trundle bed
    How many I espy
Whose nightgowns could not hide the wings,
    Although I heard them try!

But then I promised ne'er to tell;
   How could I break my word?
So go your way and I 'll go mine, —
   No fear you 'll miss the road.

IX.

MORNING is the place for dew,
    Corn is made at noon,
After dinner light for flowers,
    Dukes for setting sun!

X.

To my quick ear the leaves conferred;
  The bushes they were bells;
I could not find a privacy
  From Nature's sentinels.

In cave if I presumed to hide,
  The walls began to tell;
Creation seemed a mighty crack
  To make me visible.

XI.

A ROSE.

A SEPAL, petal, and a thorn
    Upon a common summer's morn,
A flash of dew, a bee or two,
A breeze
A caper in the trees, —
    And I 'm a rose!

XII.

HIGH from the earth I heard a bird;
  He trod upon the trees
As he esteemed them trifles,
  And then he spied a breeze,
And situated softly
  Upon a pile of wind
Which in a perturbation
  Nature had left behind.
A joyous-going fellow
  I gathered from his talk,
Which both of benediction
  And badinage partook,
Without apparent burden,
  I learned, in leafy wood
He was the faithful father
  Of a dependent brood;
And this untoward transport
  His remedy for care, —
A contrast to our respites.
  How different we are!

XIII.

COBWEBS.

THE spider as an artist
   Has never been employed
Though his surpassing merit
   Is freely certified

By every broom and Bridget
   Throughout a Christian land.
Neglected son of genius,
   I take thee by the hand.

XIV.

A WELL.

WHAT mystery pervades a well!
  The water lives so far,
Like neighbor from another world
  Residing in a jar.

The grass does not appear afraid;
  I often wonder he
Can stand so close and look so bold
  At what is dread to me.

Related somehow they may be, —
  The sedge stands next the sea,
Where he is floorless, yet of fear
  No evidence gives he.

But nature is a stranger yet;
  The ones that cite her most
Have never passed her haunted house,
  Nor simplified her ghost.

To pity those that know her not
  Is helped by the regret
That those who know her, know her less
  The nearer her they get.

XV.

To make a prairie it takes a clover
  and one bee, —
One clover, and a bee,
And revery.
The revery alone will do
If bees are few.

XVI.

THE WIND.

It's like the light, —
　A fashionless delight
It's like the bee, —
　A dateless melody.

It's like the woods,
　Private like breeze,
Phraseless, yet it stirs
　The proudest trees.

It's like the morning, —
　Best when it's done, —
The everlasting clocks
　Chime noon.

XVII.

A DEW sufficed itself
   And satisfied a leaf,
And felt, 'how vast a destiny!
   How trivial is life!'

The sun went out to work,
   The day went out to play,
But not again that dew was seen
   By physiognomy.

Whether by day abducted,
   Or emptied by the sun
Into the sea, in passing,
   Eternally unknown.

XVIII.

THE WOODPECKER.

HIS bill an auger is,
    His head, a cap and frill.
He laboreth at every tree,—
    A worm his utmost goal.

XIX.

A SNAKE.

SWEET is the swamp with its secrets,
    Until we meet a snake;
'T is then we sigh for houses,
    And our departure take
At that enthralling gallop
    That only childhood knows.
A snake is summer's treason,
    And guile is where it goes.

XX.

Could I but ride indefinite,
    As doth the meadow-bee,
And visit only where I liked,
    And no man visit me,

And flirt all day with buttercups,
    And marry whom I may,
And dwell a little everywhere,
    Or better, run away

With no police to follow,
    Or chase me if I do,
Till I should jump peninsulas
    To get away from you, —

I said, but just to be a bee
    Upon a raft of air,
And row in nowhere all day long,
    And anchor off the bar, —
What liberty! So captives deem
    Who tight in dungeons are.

XXI.

THE MOON.

THE moon was but a chin of gold
    A night or two ago,
And now she turns her perfect face
    Upon the world below.

Her forehead is of amplest blond;
    Her cheek like beryl stone;
Her eye unto the summer dew
    The likest I have known.

Her lips of amber never part;
    But what must be the smile
Upon her friend she could bestow
    Were such her silver will!

And what a privilege to be
    But the remotest star!
For certainly her way might pass
    Beside your twinkling door.

Her bonnet is the firmament,
The universe her shoe,
The stars the trinkets at her belt,
Her dimities of blue.

XXII.

THE BAT.

THE bat is dun with wrinkled wings
  Like fallow article,
And not a song pervades his lips,
  Or none perceptible.

His small umbrella, quaintly halved,
  Describing in the air
An arc alike inscrutable, —
  Elate philosopher!

Deputed from what firmament
  Of what astute abode,
Empowered with what malevolence
  Auspiciously withheld.

To his adroit Creator
  Ascribe no less the praise;
Beneficent, believe me,
  His eccentricities.

XXIII.

THE BALLOON.

YOU 've seen balloons set, have n't you?
    So stately they ascend
It is as swans discarded you
    For duties diamond.

Their liquid feet go softly out
    Upon a sea of blond;
They spurn the air as 't were too mean
    For creatures so renowned.

Their ribbons just beyond the eye,
    They struggle some for breath,
And yet the crowd applauds below;
    They would not encore death.

The gilded creature strains and spins,
    Trips frantic in a tree,
Tears open her imperial veins
    And tumbles in the sea.

The crowd retire with an oath
  The dust in streets goes down,
And clerks in counting-rooms observe,
  ' 'T was only a balloon.'

XXIV.

EVENING.

THE cricket sang,
   And set the sun,
And workmen finished, one by one,
   Their seam the day upon.

The low grass loaded with the dew,
The twilight stood as strangers do
With hat in hand, polite and new,
   To stay as if, or go.

A vastness, as a neighbor, came, —
A wisdom without face or name,
A peace, as hemispheres at home, —
   And so the night became.

XXV.

COCOON.

DRAB habitation of whom?
    Tabernacle or tomb,
Or dome of worm,
Or porch of gnome,
Or some elf's catacomb?

XXVI.

SUNSET.

A SLOOP of amber slips away
    Upon an ether sea,
And wrecks in peace a purple tar,
    The son of ecstasy.

XXVII.

AURORA.

OF bronze and blaze
    The north, to-night!
So adequate its forms,
So preconcerted with itself,
    So distant to alarms, —
An unconcern so sovereign
    To universe, or me,
It paints my simple spirit
    With tints of majesty,
Till I take vaster attitudes,
    And strut upon my stem,
Disdaining men and oxygen,
    For arrogance of them.

My splendors are menagerie;
    But their competeless show
Will entertain the centuries
    When I am, long ago,
An island in dishonored grass,
    Whom none but daisies know.

XXVIII.

THE COMING OF NIGHT.

HOW the old mountains drip with sunset,
    And the brake of dun!
How the hemlocks are tipped in tinsel
    By the wizard sun!

How the old steeples hand the scarlet,
    Till the ball is full, —
Have I the lip of the flamingo
    That I dare to tell?

Then, how the fire ebbs like billows,
    Touching all the grass
With a departing, sapphire feature,
    As if a duchess pass!

How a small dusk crawls on the village
    Till the houses blot;
And the odd flambeaux no men carry
    Glimmer on the spot!

Now it is night in nest and kennel,
   And where was the wood,
Just a dome of abyss is nodding
   Into solitude ! —

These are the visions baffled Guido ;
   Titian never told ;
Domenichino dropped the pencil,
   Powerless to unfold.

XXIX.

AFTERMATH.

THE murmuring of bees has ceased;
    But murmuring of some
Posterior, prophetic,
    Has simultaneous come, —

The lower metres of the year,
    When nature's laugh is done, —
The Revelations of the book
    Whose Genesis is June.

IV.

TIME AND ETERNITY.

I.

THIS world is not conclusion;
  A sequel stands beyond,
Invisible, as music,
  But positive, as sound.
It beckons and it baffles;
  Philosophies don't know,
And through a riddle, at the last,
  Sagacity must go.
To guess it puzzles scholars;
  To gain it, men have shown
Contempt of generations,
  And crucifixion known.

II.

WE learn in the retreating
    How vast an one
Was recently among us.
    A perished sun

Endears in the departure
    How doubly more
Than all the golden presence
    It was before!

III.

THEY say that 'time assuages,' —
   Time never did assuage;
An actual suffering strengthens,
   As sinews do, with age.

Time is a test of trouble,
   But not a remedy.
If such it prove, it prove too
   There was no malady.

IV.

We cover thee, sweet face.
  Not that we tire of thee,
But that thyself fatigue of us;
  Remember, as thou flee,
We follow thee until
  Thou notice us no more,
And then, reluctant, turn away
  To con thee o'er and o'er,
And blame the scanty love
  We were content to show,
Augmented, sweet, a hundred fold
  If thou would'st take it now.

V.

ENDING.

THAT is solemn we have ended, —
  Be it but a play,
Or a glee among the garrets,
  Or a holiday,

Or a leaving home; or later,
  Parting with a world
We have understood, for better
  Still it be unfurled.

VI.

THE stimulus, beyond the grave
His countenance to see,
Supports me like imperial drams
Afforded royally.

VII.

GIVEN in marriage unto thee,
  Oh, thou celestial host!
Bride of the Father and the Son,
  Bride of the Holy Ghost!

Other betrothal shall dissolve,
  Wedlock of will decay;
Only the keeper of this seal
  Conquers mortality.

VIII.

That such have died enables us
  The tranquiller to die;
That such have lived, certificate
  For immortality.

IX.

THEY won't frown always, — some sweet day
   When I forget to tease,
They 'll recollect how cold I looked,
   And how I just said 'please.'

Then they will hasten to the door
   To call the little child,
Who cannot thank them, for the ice
   That on her lisping piled.

X.

IMMORTALITY.

IT is an honorable thought,
    And makes one lift one's hat,
As one encountered gentlefolk
    Upon a daily street,

That we 've immortal place,
    Though pyramids decay,
And kingdoms, like the orchard,
    Flit russetly away.

XI.

THE distance that the dead have gone
  Does not at first appear;
Their coming back seems possible
  For many an ardent year.

And then, that we have followed them
  We more than half suspect,
So intimate have we become
  With their dear retrospect.

XII.

How dare the robins sing,
    When men and women hear
Who since they went to their account
    Have settled with the year! —
Paid all that life had earned
    In one consummate bill,
And now, what life or death can do
    Is immaterial.
Insulting is the sun
    To him whose mortal light,
Beguiled of immortality,
    Bequeaths him to the night.
In deference to him
    Extinct be every hum,
Whose garden wrestles with the dew,
    At daybreak overcome!

XIII.

DEATH.

DEATH is like the insect
    Menacing the tree,
Competent to kill it,
    But decoyed may be.

Bait it with the balsam,
    Seek it with the knife,
Baffle, if it cost you
    Everything in life.

Then, if it have burrowed
    Out of reach of skill,
Ring the tree and leave it, —
    'T is the vermin's will.

XIV.

UNWARNED.

'T IS sunrise, little maid, hast thou
    No station in the day?
'T was not thy wont to hinder so, —
    Retrieve thine industry.

'T is noon, my little maid, alas!
    And art thou sleeping yet?
The lily waiting to be wed,
    The bee, dost thou forget?

My little maid, 't is night; alas,
    That night should be to thee
Instead of morning! Hadst thou broached
    Thy little plan to me,
Dissuade thee if I could not, sweet,
    I might have aided thee.

XV.

EACH that we lose takes part of us;
   A crescent still abides,
Which like the moon, some turbid night,
   Is summoned by the tides.

XVI.

Not any higher stands the grave
    For heroes than for men;
Not any nearer for the child
    Than numb three-score and ten.

This latest leisure equal lulls
    The beggar and his queen;
Propitiate this democrat
    By summer's gracious mien.

XVII.

ASLEEP.

As far from pity as complaint,
   As cool to speech as stone,
As numb to revelation
   As if my trade were bone.

As far from time as history,
   As near yourself to-day
As children to the rainbow's scarf,
   Or sunset's yellow play

To eyelids in the sepulchre.
   How still the dancer lies,
While color's revelations break,
   And blaze the butterflies!

XVIII.

THE SPIRIT.

'TIS whiter than an Indian pipe,
  'T is dimmer than a lace;
No stature has it, like a fog,
  When you approach the place.

Not any voice denotes it here,
  Or intimates it there;
A spirit, how doth it accost?
  What customs hath the air?

This limitless hyperbole
  Each one of us shall be;
'T is drama, if (hypothesis)
  It be not tragedy!

XIX.

THE MONUMENT.

SHE laid her docile crescent down,
   And this mechanic stone
Still states, to dates that have forgot,
   The news that she is gone.

So constant to its stolid trust,
   The shaft that never knew,
It shames the constancy that fled
   Before its emblem flew.

XX.

BLESS God, he went as soldiers,
  His musket on his breast;
Grant, God, he charge the bravest
  Of all the martial blest.

Please God, might I behold him
  In epauletted white,
I should not fear the foe then,
  I should not fear the fight.

XXI.

IMMORTAL is an ample word
  When what we need is by,
But when it leaves us for a time,
  'T is a necessity.

Of heaven above the firmest proof
  We fundamental know,
Except for its marauding hand,
  It had been heaven below.

XXII.

WHERE every bird is bold to go,
    And bees abashless play,
The foreigner before he knocks
    Must thrust the tears away.

XXIII.

THE grave my little cottage is,
  Where, keeping house for thee,
I make my parlor orderly,
  And lay the marble tea,

For two divided, briefly,
  A cycle, it may be,
Till everlasting life unite
  In strong society.

XXIV.

THIS was in the white of the year,
    That was in the green,
Drifts were as difficult then to think
    As daisies now to be seen.

Looking back is best that is left,
    Or if it be before,
Retrospection is prospect's half,
    Sometimes almost more.

XXV.

SWEET hours have perished here;
   This is a mighty room;
Within its precincts hopes have played, —
Now shadows in the tomb.

XXVI.

ME! Come! My dazzled face
In such a shining place!

Me! Hear! My foreign ear
The sounds of welcome near!

The saints shall meet
Our bashful feet.

My holiday shall be
That they remember me;

My paradise, the fame
That they pronounce my name.

XXVII.

INVISIBLE.

FROM us she wandered now a year,
    Her tarrying unknown;
If wilderness prevent her feet,
    Or that ethereal zone

No eye hath seen and lived,
    We ignorant must be.
We only know what time of year
    We took the mystery.

XXVIII.

I WISH I knew that woman's name,
　　So, when she comes this way,
To hold my life, and hold my ears,
　　For fear I hear her say

She 's 'sorry I am dead,' again,
　　Just when the grave and I
Have sobbed ourselves almost to sleep, —
　　Our only lullaby.

XXIX.

TRYING TO FORGET.

BEREAVED of all, I went abroad,
    No less bereaved to be
Upon a new peninsula, —
    The grave preceded me,

Obtained my lodgings ere myself,
    And when I sought my bed,
The grave it was, reposed upon
    The pillow for my head.

I waked, to find it first awake,
    I rose, — it followed me;
I tried to drop it in the crowd,
    To lose it in the sea,

In cups of artificial drowse
    To sleep its shape away, —
The grave was finished, but the spade
    Remained in memory.

XXX.

I FELT a funeral in my brain,
    And mourners, to and fro,
Kept treading, treading, till it seemed
    That sense was breaking through.

And when they all were seated,
    A service like a drum
Kept beating, beating, till I thought
    My mind was going numb.

And then I heard them lift a box,
    And creak across my soul
With those same boots of lead, again.
    Then space began to toll

As all the heavens were a bell,
    And Being but an ear,
And I and silence some strange race,
    Wrecked, solitary, here.

XXXI.

I MEANT to find her when I came;
   Death had the same design;
But the success was his, it seems,
   And the discomfit mine.

I meant to tell her how I longed
   For just this single time;
But Death had told her so the first,
   And she had hearkened him.

To wander now is my abode;
   To rest, — to rest would be
A privilege of hurricane
   To memory and me.

XXXII.

WAITING.

I SING to use the waiting,
   My bonnet but to tie,
And shut the door unto my house;
   No more to do have I,

Till, his best step approaching,
   We journey to the day,
And tell each other how we sang
   To keep the dark away.

XXXIII.

A SICKNESS of this world it most occasions
    When best men die;
A wishfulness their far condition
    To occupy.

A chief indifference, as foreign
    A world must be
Themselves forsake contented,
    For Deity.

XXXIV.

SUPERFLUOUS were the sun
    When excellence is dead;
He were superfluous every day,
    For every day is said

That syllable whose faith
    Just saves it from despair,
And whose 'I'll meet you' hesitates
    If love inquire, 'Where?'

Upon his dateless fame
    Our periods may lie,
As stars that drop anonymous
    From an abundant sky.

XXXV.

So proud she was to die
   It made us all ashamed
That what we cherished, so unknown
   To her desire seemed.

So satisfied to go
   Where none of us should be,
Immediately, that anguish stooped
   Almost to jealousy.

XXXVI.

FAREWELL.

TIE the strings to my life, my Lord,
    Then I am ready to go!
Just a look at the horses —
    Rapid! That will do!

Put me in on the firmest side,
    So I shall never fall;
For we must ride to the Judgment,
    And it's partly down hill.

But never I mind the bridges,
    And never I mind the sea;
Held fast in everlasting race
    By my own choice and thee.

Good-by to the life I used to live,
    And the world I used to know;
And kiss the hills for me, just once;
    Now I am ready to go!

XXXVII.

THE dying need but little, dear, —
    A glass of water's all,
A flower's unobtrusive face
    To punctuate the wall,

A fan, perhaps, a friend's regret,
    And certainly that one
No color in the rainbow
    Perceives when you are gone.

XXXVIII.

DEAD.

There's something quieter than sleep
    Within this inner room !
It wears a sprig upon its breast,
    And will not tell its name.

Some touch it and some kiss it,
    Some chafe its idle hand ;
It has a simple gravity
    I do not understand !

While simple-hearted neighbors
    Chat of the 'early dead,'
We, prone to periphrasis,
    Remark that birds have fled !

XXXIX.

THE soul should always stand ajar,
  That if the heaven inquire,
He will not be obliged to wait,
  Or shy of troubling her.

Depart, before the host has slid
  The bolt upon the door,
To seek for the accomplished guest, —
  Her visitor no more.

XL.

THREE weeks passed since I had seen her, —
    Some disease had vexed;
'T was with text and village singing
    I beheld her next,

And a company — our pleasure
    To discourse alone;
Gracious now to me as any,
    Gracious unto none.

Borne, without dissent of either,
    To the parish night;
Of the separated people
    Which are out of sight?

XLI.

I BREATHED enough to learn the trick,
    And now, removed from air,
I simulate the breath so well,
    That one, to be quite sure

The lungs are stirless, must descend
    Among the cunning cells,
And touch the pantomime himself.
    How cool the bellows feels!

XLII.

I WONDER if the sepulchre
  Is not a lonesome way,
When men and boys, and larks and June
Go down the fields to hay!

XLIII.

JOY IN DEATH.

IF tolling bell I ask the cause.
   'A soul has gone to God,'
I'm answered in a lonesome tone;
   Is heaven then so sad?

That bells should joyful ring to tell
   A soul had gone to heaven,
Would seem to me the proper way
   A good news should be given.

XLIV.

IF I may have it when it's dead
    I will contented be;
If just as soon as breath is out
    It shall belong to me,

Until they lock it in the grave,
    'T is bliss I cannot weigh,
For though they lock thee in the grave,
    Myself can hold the key.

Think of it, lover! I and thee
    Permitted face to face to be;
After a life, a death we'll say, —
    For death was that, and this is thee.

XLV.

BEFORE the ice is in the pools,
  Before the skaters go,
Or any cheek at nightfall
  Is tarnished by the snow,

Before the fields have finished,
  Before the Christmas tree,
Wonder upon wonder
  Will arrive to me!

What we touch the hems of
  On a summer's day;
What is only walking
  Just a bridge away;

That which sings so, speaks so,
  When there's no one here, —
Will the frock I wept in
  Answer me to wear?

XLVI.

DYING.

I HEARD a fly buzz when I died;
  The stillness round my form
Was like the stillness in the air
  Between the heaves of storm.

The eyes beside had wrung them dry,
  And breaths were gathering sure
For that last onset, when the king
  Be witnessed in his power.

I willed my keepsakes, signed away
  What portion of me I
Could make assignable, — and then
  There interposed a fly,

With blue, uncertain, stumbling buzz,
  Between the light and me;
And then the windows failed, and then
  I could not see to see.

XLVII.

A DRIFT! A little boat adrift!
And night is coming down!
Will no one guide a little boat
   Unto the nearest town?

So sailors say, on yesterday,
   Just as the dusk was brown,
One little boat gave up its strife,
   And gurgled down and down.

But angels say, on yesterday,
   Just as the dawn was red,
One little boat o'erspent with gales
Retrimmed its masts, redecked its sails
   Exultant, onward sped!

XLVIII.

THERE's been a death in the opposite house
    As lately as to-day.
I know it by the numb look
    Such houses have alway.

The neighbors rustle in and out,
    The doctor drives away.
A window opens like a pod,
    Abrupt, mechanically;

Somebody flings a mattress out, —
    The children hurry by;
They wonder if It died on that, —
    I used to when a boy.

The minister goes stiffly in
    As if the house were his,
And he owned all the mourners now,
    And little boys besides;

And then the milliner, and the man
   Of the appalling trade,
To take the measure of the house.
   There'll be that dark parade

Of tassels and of coaches soon;
   It's easy as a sign, —
The intuition of the news
   In just a country town.

XLIX.

WE never know we go, — when we are going
   We jest and shut the door;
Fate following behind us bolts it,
  And we accost no more.

L.

THE SOUL'S STORM.

IT struck me every day
    The lightning was as new
As if the cloud that instant slit
    And let the fire through.

It burned me in the night,
    It blistered in my dream;
It sickened fresh upon my sight
    With every morning's beam.

I thought that storm was brief, —
    The maddest, quickest by;
But Nature lost the date of this,
    And left it in the sky.

LI.

WATER is taught by thirst;
    Land, by the oceans passed;
Transport, by throe;
Peace, by its battles told;
Love, by memorial mould;
    Birds, by the snow.

LII.

THIRST.

WE thirst at first, — 't is Nature's act;
    And later, when we die,
A little water supplicate
    Of fingers going by.

It intimates the finer want,
    Whose adequate supply
Is that great water in the west
    Termed immortality.

LIII.

A CLOCK stopped — not the mantel's;
    Geneva's farthest skill
Can't put the puppet bowing
    That just now dangled still.

An awe came on the trinket!
    The figures hunched with pain,
Then quivered out of decimals
    Into degreeless noon.

It will not stir for doctors,
    This pendulum of snow;
The shopman importunes it,
    While cool, concernless No

Nods from the gilded pointers,
    Nods from the seconds slim,
Decades of arrogance between
    The dial life and him.

LIV.

CHARLOTTE BRONTË'S GRAVE.

ALL overgrown by cunning moss,
   All interspersed with weed,
The little cage of 'Currer Bell,'
   In quiet Haworth laid.

This bird, observing others,
   When frosts too sharp became,
Retire to other latitudes,
   Quietly did the same,

But differed in returning;
   Since Yorkshire hills are green,
Yet not in all the nests I meet
   Can nightingale be seen.

Gathered from many wanderings,
   Gethsemane can tell
Through what transporting anguish
   She reached the asphodel!

Soft fall the sounds of Eden
   Upon her puzzled ear ;
Oh, what an afternoon for heaven,
   When ' Brontë ' entered there !

LV.

A TOAD can die of light!
Death is the common right
Of toads and men, —
Of earl and midge
The privilege.
Why swagger then?
The gnat's supremacy
Is large as thine.

LVI.

Far from love the Heavenly Father
  Leads the chosen child;
Oftener through realm of briar
  Than the meadow mild,

Oftener by the claw of dragon
  Than the hand of friend,
Guides the little one predestined
  To the native land.

LVII.

SLEEPING.

A LONG, long sleep, a famous sleep
   That makes no show for dawn
By stretch of limb or stir of lid, —
   An independent one.

Was ever idleness like this?
   Within a hut of stone
To bask the centuries away
   Nor once look up for noon?

LVIII.

RETROSPECT.

'TWAS just this time last year I died.
    I know I heard the corn,
When I was carried by the farms, —
    It had the tassels on.

I thought how yellow it would look
    When Richard went to mill;
And then I wanted to get out,
    But something held my will.

I thought just how red apples wedged
    The stubble's joints between;
And carts went stooping round the fields
    To take the pumpkins in.

I wondered which would miss me least,
    And when Thanksgiving came,
If father 'd multiply the plates
    To make an even sum.

And if my stocking hung too high,
　Would it blur the Christmas glee,
That not a Santa Claus could reach
　The altitude of me?

But this sort grieved myself, and so
　I thought how it would be
When just this time, some perfect year,
　Themselves should come to me.

LIX.

ETERNITY.

On this wondrous sea,
   Sailing silently,
Ho! pilot, ho!
Knowest thou the shore
Where no breakers roar,
   Where the storm is o'er?

In the silent west
Many sails at rest,
   Their anchors fast;
Thither I pilot thee, —
Land, ho! Eternity!
   Ashore at last!

www.ingramcontent.com/pod-product-compliance
Lightning Source LLC
Chambersburg PA
CBHW020910230426
43666CB00008B/1387